MICHELLE OBAMA biography bio book

by David Right

PREFACE

Black women have always been an indispensable and fundamental bridge connecting, the elements and conditions of every day living to purpose, strength and determination. Working women were confirmed by the Feminist Movement that is it okay to be every woman successfully juggling multiple roles of wife, mother, caregiver and career while negotiating the obstacles of race, class and gender.

In the past decade, there have been phenomenal achievements by Black women as Entrepreneurs Scientists, roles in technology, in the board room as executives, in many areas as athletes, world famous entertainers, television talk show hosts, moguls and actors in spite of socioeconomic indicators showing that Black women are still straggling to catch up to their White counterparts.

A woman's role today can be defined as a stay-at-home/work-at-home entrepreneur or a single working mother with a high powered corporate title trophy wife defined as a symbol of success and prowess being sought out by high powered men. Women have broken through the old barriers of sexism all the way to the White House.

The First Lady, Michelle Obama has inspired women in many ways to make a new commitment to the way they live. Living life on purpose and not by accident allows no room for excuses to be mediocre. Everyday for eight years and many years to come black children, black girls, black women will see a positive, honest, image of a woman who looks like them explode and redefine the negative myths about women of color.

A strong woman that makes no excuses for how she defines herself in the role of individual first, friend/partner to her husband and mother. Mrs. Obama takes all of her roles seriously and you can see this in her eyes, hear it in the conviction of her words when she speaks. She is so fortunate to have been able to rely on her mother to take care of her children, it undoubtedly gave her a sense of peace that no one else could have provided for her. We know that our mother will take care our children the way we would or better.

There is no misrepresentation for acceptable definitions of Black women that I can see when it comes to Michelle Obama. She sends a message to the world saying it is more than okay to be to be dark-skinned, to be smart, to be tall, to be different and most of all to be the First Lady of African American descent in the White House. The tremendous amount of pressure of being in the public view, constantly having everything you do reported on every minute of every day. Constant travel and movement, speaking to thousands of people at a time did not cause her to compromise the level of care for herself first, her husband and their children.

Table of Contents

CHAPTER 1- THE BIOGRAPHY OF MICHELLE OBAMA

Michelle Obama was the 44th first lady of the United States and wife of U.S. President Barack Obama. Prior to her role as first lady, she was a lawyer, Chicago city administrator and community-outreach worker.

"Every day, the people I meet inspire me, every day they make me proud, every day they remind me how blessed we are to live in the greatest nation on Earth. Serving as your first lady is an honor and a privilege."

—Michelle Obama

Synopsis

Michelle Obama was born on January 17, 1964, in Chicago, Illinois. She attended Princeton University, graduating cum laude in 1985, and went on to earn a degree from Harvard Law School in 1988. Following her graduation from Harvard, she worked at a Chicago law firm, where she met her husband, future U.S. president Barack Obama. The couple married on October 3, 1992. As first lady, she focused her attention on current social issues, such as poverty, healthy living, and education.

Background and Early Life

Michelle Obama was born Michelle LaVaughn Robinson on January 17, 1964, in Chicago, Illinois. She would later become a lawyer, Chicago city administrator, community-outreach worker and—as the wife of President Barack Obama—the first African-American first lady of the United States.

Michelle was raised in a small bungalow on Chicago's South Side. Her father, Fraser Robinson, was a city-pump operator and a Democratic precinct captain. Her mother, Marian, was a secretary at Spiegel's but later stayed home to raise Michelle and her older brother, Craig. They were a close-knit family, typically sharing meals, reading and playing games together.

Craig and Michelle, 21 months apart in age, were often mistaken for twins. The siblings also shared close quarters, sleeping in the living room with a sheet serving as a makeshift room divider. They were raised with an emphasis on education and had learned to read at home by age four. Both skipped the second grade.

Gifted Student

By the sixth grade, Michelle was taking classes in her school's gifted program, where she learned French and completed accelerated courses in biology. She went on to attend Whitney M. Young Magnet High School, the city's first magnet high school for gifted children, where, among other activities, she served as the student government treasurer. In 1981, Michelle graduated from the school as class salutatorian.

Following in her older brother's footsteps, Michelle then attended Princeton University, graduating cum laude in 1985 with a B.A. in Sociology. She went on to study law at Harvard Law School, where she took part in demonstrations calling for the enrollment and hiring of more minority students and professors. She was awarded her J.D. in 1988.

Marriage to Barack Obama

After law school, Michelle worked as an associate in the Chicago branch of the firm Sidley Austin, in the area of marketing and intellectual property. It was there, in 1989, that she met her future husband, Barack Obama, a summer intern to whom she was assigned as an adviser.

Initially, she refused to date Barack, believing that their work relationship would make the romance improper. She eventually relented, however, and the couple soon fell in love.

Did You Know? The Obamas' first kiss took place outside of a Chicago shopping center—where a pla☐ue featuring a photo of the couple kissing was installed more than two decades later, in August 2012.

After two years of dating, Barack proposed, and the couple married at Trinity United Church of Christ on October 3, 1992. Their daughters, Malia and Sasha, were born in 1998 and 2001, respectively.

High-Profile Work in Chicago

In 1991, Michelle decided to leave corporate law and pursue a career in public service, working as an assistant to Mayor Richard Daley and then as the assistant commissioner of planning and development for the City of Chicago.

In 1993, she became executive director for the Chicago office of Public Allies, a nonprofit leadership-training program that helped young adults develop skills for future careers in the public sector.

In 1996, Michelle joined the University of Chicago as associate dean of student services, developing the school's first community-service program. Beginning in 2002, she worked for the University of Chicago Hospitals, as executive director of community relations and external affairs.

In May 2005, Michelle was appointed vice president for community and external affairs at the University of Chicago Medical Center, where she continued to work part-time until shortly before her husband's inauguration as president. She also served as a board member for the prestigious Chicago Council on Global Affairs.

On the Campaign Trail

Michelle Obama first caught the eye of a national audience while at her husband's side when he delivered a high-profile speech at the Democratic National Convention in 2004. Barack Obama was elected as U.S. Senator from Illinois that November.

In 2007, Michelle scaled back her own professional work to attend to family and campaign obligations during Barack's run for the Democratic presidential nomination. When they were out on the trail, they would leave their daughters with their grandmother Marian, Michelle's mother. Barack Obama eventually won the nomination and was elected the 44th President of the United States. He was sworn in on January 20, 2009.

When her husband sought reelection in 2012, facing a challenging race against Republican presidential nominee Mitt Romney, Michelle Obama diligently campaigned on his behalf. She traveled the country, giving talks and making public appearances.

In September of that year, Michelle delivered a noteworthy speech at the Democratic National Convention. "Every day, the people I meet inspire me, every day they make me proud, every day they remind me how blessed we are to live in the greatest nation on earth," she said. "Serving as your first lady is an honor and a privilege." She went on to praise the Latino community for supporting President Obama, and stated that her husband—"the same man she fell in love with all those years ago"—understands the American Dream, as well as the everyday struggles of American families, and cares deeply about making a difference in people's lives. Michelle won both public and critical praise for her narrative called a "shining moment" by The Washington Post.

On November 6, 2012, Barack Obama was reelected for a second term as U.S. president. After Mitt Romney conceded defeat, Michelle Obama accompanied her husband with their two daughters, Malia and Sasha, onto the stage at McCormick Place in Chicago, where President Obama delivered his victory speech.

Fashion Icon

After her husband's political role pushed the Obama family into the spotlight, Michelle was publicly recognized for her no-nonsense campaign style as well as her sense of fashion. In May 2006, Michelle was featured in Essence magazine as one of "25 of the World's Most Inspiring Women." In September 2007, Michelle was included in 02138 magazine as number 58 in "The Harvard 100," a yearly list of the school's most influential alumni. She has also twice appeared on the cover of Vogue and made the Vanity Fair best-dressed list two years in a row as well as People magazine's 2008 best-dressed list.

During the inauguration ceremony for her husband's second term, on January 21, 2013, Michelle and her daughters received alot of attention for their fashion choices, which included clothes from Thom Browne, J. Crew and Kate Spade. Michelle received much praise for the red Jason Wu dress she wore during the subse□uent events.

Issues and Causes

As the 44th first lady of the United States, Michelle Obama has focused her attention on issues such as the support of military families, helping working women balance career and family and encouraging national service. During the first year of the Obama presidency, Michelle and her husband volunteered at homeless shelters and soup kitchens in the Washington D.C. area. Michelle also has made appearances at public schools, stressing the importance of education and volunteer work.

Ever conscious of her family's diet and health, Michelle has supported the organic-food movement, instructing the White House kitchens to prepare organic food for guests and her family. In March 2009, Michelle worked with 23 fifth graders from a local school in Washington D.C. to plant an 1,100-s□uare-foot garden of fresh vegetables and install beehives on the South Lawn of the White House. Since 2010, Michelle has put efforts to fight childhood obesity near the top of her agenda.

Michelle Obama remains committed to her health-and-wellness causes. In 2012, she announced a new fitness program for kids as part of her Let's Move initiative. Along with the U.S. Olympic team and other sports organizations, she has worked to get young people to try out a new sport or activity. "That year, 1.7 million young people participated in Olympic and Paralympic sports in their communities—many of them for the very first time. And that is so important, because sometimes all it takes is that first lesson, or clinic, or class to get a child excited about a new sport," she said in a statement.

Putting her message in print, Michelle released a book as part of her mission to promote healthy eating. American Grown: The Story of the White House Kitchen Garden and Gardens Across America (2012) explores her own experience creating a vegetable garden as well as the work of community gardens elsewhere. She told Reuters that sees the book as an opportunity to help readers understand "where their food was coming from" and "to talk about the work that we're doing with childhood obesity and childhood health."

Powerful Speeches

In July 2016, former first lady, senator and secretary of state Hillary Clinton became the official Democratic nominee for the American presidency, becoming the first woman in the U.S. to win a major political party's presidential nomination. On the first night of the Democratic National Convention, Michelle spoke in support of Clinton, who had previously run against Barack Obama during the 2008 primaries, and her vision of a progressive America.

"...I wake up every morning in a house that was built by slaves, and I watch my daughters, two beautiful, intelligent, black young women, playing with their dogs on the White House lawn," she said. "And because of Hillary Clinton, my daughters, and all our sons and daughters, now take for granted that a woman can be president of the United States."

Obama continued to campaign for Clinton, speaking out forcefully against the campaign of Republican candidate Donald Trump, who went on to win the presidential election.

On January 13, 2017, Obama made her final speech as First lady at the White House, saying "being your first lady has been the greatest honor of my life and I hope I've made you proud."

In an emotional moment, she addressed young Americans: "I want our young people to know that they matter, that they belong. So don't be afraid. You hear me, young people? Don't be afraid. Be focused. Be determined. Be hopeful. Be empowered. Empower yourself with a good education. Then get out there and use that education to build a country worthy of your boundless promise. Lead by example with hope; never fear."

First Family

Both Michelle and Barack Obama have stated that their personal priority is their two daughters, Malia and Sasha. The parents realized that the move from Chicago to Washington D.C. would be a major adjustment for any family. Residing in the White House, having Secret Service protection and always being in the wake of their parents' public obligations has dramatically transformed their lives. Both parents try to make their daughters' world as "normal" as possible, with set times for studying, going to bed and getting up. "My first priority will always be to make sure that our girls are healthy and grounded," Michelle said. "Then I want to help other families get the support they need, not just to survive, but to thrive."

CHAPTER 2- HOW SHE MET BARACK OBAM

Going back to the public marriage records of President Obama in 1992, Mac Arthur commented "people understood that putting the two of them together is like putting hydrogen and oxygen together to create the unbelievable life force" (Carol Felsenthal 'The making of the first lady' Chicago Mag.com2/2009) and indeed a life force they are with their commitment, love and friendship towards each other. They are living examples of those rare people who are still happy and content in institutional marriage when humanity shifts to decadence through turbulent times.

When Michelle first saw the new intern who walked in her plush downtown Chicago law firm one summer morning, she must not have dreamt that this lanky, sharp featured youth would be the world's most powerful man in the making. As an associate from the Harvard, Obama joined the firm to get hands on experience in corporate law and Michelle was his tutor.

From the very beginning Michelle could feel the young man showed more interest in her than in law, but the intelligent sociology major form Princeton University was not interested. Born on 17th Jan 1964 and having had her childhood in a modest one bedroom house in Chicago, she invested time and energy in running literacy programs, recruiting minority undergraduates in Harvard and initiating social changes for betterment. In 1985, after graduating from the university with Cum Laude honors, she joined Harvard and achieved a law degree in 1988, a year prior to Barack and though they attended the same college, they never before met each other. Initially, Barack Hussein Obama's advances were not reciprocated by Michelle Robinson, however finally cupid hit the bull's eye and they fell deeply in love with each other. In her own words, she was in love with him "for the same reason many other people respect him; his connection with people".

On their first date, they sauntered to art institute and picked up lunch later at a café, then went for the movie "Do the right thing" followed by a drink in the John Hancock building, 99th floor. Finally in 1992 the two got married and Michelle says in retrospect "He swept me off my feet".

Their public marriage records are available in many websites but some of these cite October 18 as their wedding date whereas some mention it as 3rd October 1992. The Trinity United Church of Chicago, Illinois has the public marriage records for this would be world famous couple secured, as the wedding took place in this church performed by Reverend Jeremiah A Wright Jr. and the reception was organized at the South Shore Cultural Centre. It was a great union of two highly energetic people filled with life force and passion to make dreams come true.

In Swahili (the primary language in Kenya), Barack means "the blessed one" and in all respect Obama personifies being blessed and alot more. With Michelle by his side providing incessant support, his brilliance dazzled, and in 2004 November he was elected as US Senator representing Illinois. By then he was a loving father of two beautiful girls and the future held much more for him.

The world witnessed his stupendous charisma during the election campaign and following shortly this charming man became the 44th President of United States of America. In spite of their extremely busy schedule day in and day out, Obama loves to spend □uality time with his wife and kids. The President himself proclaimed unabashedly in front of the entire world the wonderful chemistry he has with Michelle. "I would not be standing here tonight without the unyielding support of my best friend for the last 16 years. The rock of our family, the love of my life, the nation's first lady...Michelle Obama". (President elect Barack Obama's remark in Chicago SFGate.com 11/4/2008).

The Obama Marriage - Friends and Lovers, Too

With all the media attention being focused on the politics of the moment, most analysts have overlooked one of the most defining characteristics of the Obama presidency: His marriage. Yet even the casual observer cannot help but notice the Obamas' friends-and-lovers-too relationship. That's the image they project whenever they are in public together.

Certainly if you are under forty years old, and you saw the Minnesota hand bump, you took it as a sign of two best buddies celebrating. We have to look deeper, however, into the American psyche to understand why people see the Barak and Michelle Obama as role modeling the ideal American marriage.

People identify with the Obama marriage because lovers, who are best friends, are the type of couple that we admire most. So we notice that the Obamas are relaxed and spontaneous when they are in the public eye. And we acknowledge that they actually are having fun together despite the demands of their positions as president and first lady. Americans also realize that they share similar goals, including raising their children in a nurturing environment. Yet their relationship goes much deeper than what we see in the video clips.

On the night that Barack and his team of advisors decided to make the run for the presidency, Michelle was there as Barack's supportive best friend. She knew him so well that she interrupted the politicking and asked him right in front of everyone what he hoped to achieve by making a run for the White House. That forced Barack to cut to the chase.

The future president pondered the thought for a moment, and then he said he wanted to make America a place where every child could fulfill his or her dream. As an afterthought, he added that every child in the world should have a similar opportunity. After hearing that, no one in the room could back out or back down. And the race was on. The team had discovered it's mission with the help of Michelle Obama, who had prodded Barack--her best friend--to either get it on or get over it--the idea of running for president. This is just one of many examples of how the Obamas' friendship relationship works in uncanny ways.

In the Obamas' pressure-cooker world, their combined social and verbal skills help them discover a shared purpose, founded on shared values. This doubles their power to make good decisions in their domestic and public life, as well as with their careers. It also gives them a common ground on which their romantic relationship is played out.

To better understand the Obama friends-and-lovers-too relationship, let's look at the ⬚ualities it contains:

- Mutual trust and cooperation
- Emotional honesty
- Encouragement for expressing one's true feelings
- An active listening processes where they hear each other out
- Support for each other's goals and emotional growth
- A collaborative helping process whereby they solve problems together
- A sense of e⬚uity that both partners really matter
- Mutual affirmation and self-validation
- Common concern and care for their children
- Supportive mutual friends
- Celebrating their successes together

That is an unusual list of qualities for a romantic relationship. Yet it shows the kinds of attributes that it takes to support a low-stress romance when you have a high-performance career.

Some people find the Obama marriage easy to imagine. Others see it as a long-term solution to the problems that they keep repeating over and over, ad infinitum, in their relationships. But if you're under twenty-six years old and single, you might be moving too fast to imagine being friends with your lovers.

Or, if you've loved and lost, and are bitter about it, you might be put off by other's successes. Still, there is alot you can learn from the example they set.

Barack and Michelle Obama show what is possible to achieve in a romantic relationship. And just because they are rich and famous, you should not take the stand that you could not do it too. You can have a relationship like the Obama marriage if you work on developing certain relationship skills.

CHAPTER 3- ACCOMPLISHMENTS AS THE FIRST LADY

As we take a look back over the last eight years, the Obama Administration has accomplished alot, and shaken some things up in order to move this country forward. But we can't forget about the accomplishments of President Obama's right hand (no, not Joe), Michelle Obama. Michelle has willingly taken on some of the most controversial issues in American history and went head to head to fight them.

Forget that this First Lady was known by the nickname of "The Closer" during campaigning because she is skilled at persuading undecided voters to sign pledge cards – closing the deal.

Forget that Michelle was named as the #1 most stylish in Style Magazine in 2013.

Forget that First Lady Michelle Obama is one of the few First Lady's to show love for her husband openly without scandal.

In the last interview with Michelle Obama as the First Lady, Oprah went over what it was really like to be in that position and live under serious scrutiny. President Obama, who briefly slid into the interview room to give his insight on the First Lady, made respect FLOTUS even more.

"You know, we all knew she was brilliant and cute and strong and a great mom," he said, "but I think the way in which she blended purpose and policy with fun so that she was able to reach beyond Washington … was masterful."

But don't hold your breath for her to run for president.

"If I were interested in it, I'd say it," she tells Winfrey. "I don't believe in playing games. It's not something I would do, but it also speaks to the fact that people don't really understand how (being in the White House) is."

"I mean, the next family that comes in here, every person in that family, every child, every grandchild, their lives will be turned upside down in a way that no American really understands," she continues. "And it's not for us to complain about it. So you don't hear complaints. But it is a — a truth, an actuality, that there is a weight to it."

"My desire for this country is that we remain hopeful and that we find a place in our hearts to love each other."

Even if you forget all of that, we've got 16 other amazing accomplishments that First Lady Michelle Obama has done. Take a look.

1. In 2010, she launched Let's Move!, bringing together community leaders, educators, medical professionals, parents, and others in a nationwide effort to address the challenge of childhood obesity. Let's Move! has an ambitious goal: to solve the epidemic of childhood obesity within a generation. Whether it's providing healthier food in our schools, helping kids be more physically active, or urging companies to market healthier foods to our children, Let's Move! is focused on giving parents the support they need to make healthier choices for their kids.

2. In 2010 she passed The School Lunch program with bipartisan support. The program provides free and reduced-price meals to more than 21 million low-income children, now re□uires districts to serve more fruit, vegetables, whole grains, lean protein and low-fat dairy products.

3. Walgreens, Supervalu, Walmart and several regional grocers announced a commitment to build or expand 1,500 stores in communities with limited or no access to healthy food. This initiative will create thousands of local jobs and will provide access to fresh food to an estimated 9.5 million people who currently have limited access. In California alone, the Fresh Works Fund has committed 200 million dollars to this effort to increase access to healthy food.

4. Darden, the world's largest full service restaurant company, which owns Olive Garden, Red Lobster and other chains, made a commitment to improve kids' menus by offering a fruit or vegetable and low-fat milk with every

meal. Darden will also reduce total calories and sodium by 20% across their menus over the next 10 years.

5. The First Lady launched MyPlate and MiPlato, an easy to understand icon to help parents make healthier choices for their families. More than 6,100 community groups and 100 national organizations and corporations have partnered with the USDA to give families across the country access to this important nutritional information.

6. The First Lady worked with the US Tennis Association to build or refurbish more than 6,200 kid-sized tennis courts across the country, sign up more than 250,000 kids to complete their PALAs, and train 12,000 coaches to help kids learn the sport of tennis.

7. The First Lady launched Let's Move! Child Care to ensure that our youngest children are getting a healthy start. As of January of 2013, more than 10,000 child care professionals and organizations have registered to implement new criteria for nutrition, physical activity, and limited screen time.

8. Walmart announced a new Nutrition Charter through which they lowered the cost of fruits, vegetables, and whole grain products by $1 billion in 2011. Wal-Mart has also pledged to work with manufacturers to eliminate trans fats and remove 10% of the sugar and 25% of the sodium in the food they sell by 2015.

9. Through Chefs Move to School, 2,400 chefs and nearly 4,000 schools have signed up to work together, teaching kids about healthy eating and helping cafeteria staff prepare healthier meals.

10. The country's largest food manufacturers pledged to cut 1.5 trillion calories from the food they sell by 25 through their Healthy Weight Commitment Foundation.

11. The American Beverage Association fulfilled their commitment to the First Lady to put clear calorie labels on the front of their products to give consumers better information.

12. Through her Let's Move! Museums and Gardens, 597 participating institutions in all 50 states and the District of Columbia have signed up to offer active exhibits and healthy food choices.

13. In 2011, Mrs. Obama and Dr. Jill Biden came together to launch Joining Forces, a nationwide initiative calling all Americans to rally around service members, veterans, and their families and support them through wellness, education, and employment opportunities. Joining Forces works hand in hand with the public and private sector to ensure that service members, veterans, and their families have the tools they need to succeed throughout their lives.

14. In 2014, Mrs. Obama launched the Reach Higher Initiative, an effort to inspire young people across America to take charge of their future by completing their education past high school, whether at a professional training program, a community college, or a four-year college or university. Reach Higher aims to ensure that all students understand what they need to complete their education by working to expose students to college and career opportunities; helping them understand financial aid eligibility; encouraging academic planning and summer learning opportunities; and supporting high school counselors who do essential work to help students get into college.

15. In 2015, Mrs. Obama joined President Obama to launch Let Girls Learn, a U.S. government-wide initiative to help girls around the world go to school and stay in school. As part of this effort, Mrs. Obama is calling on countries across the globe to help educate and empower young women, and she is sharing the stories and struggles of these young women with young people here at home to inspire them to commit to their own education.

16. Michelle hosted a White House dinner to support mentoring programs for young girls, encouraging them to break the glass ceiling. "Once you see somebody on TV it looks like it's easy, but the truth is we only know many of these women once they've become famous, once they're in the news. Faith and love and hard work — that's what got us through. You don't need money or connections. The ☐uestion is, do you let that fear stop you?"

Even while her husband's approval rating by the American public has fluctuated, Michelle's has stayed surprisingly high. In August 2011, President Barack Obama's approval rating plummeted to 40%, but Michelle's remained high at 70%.

Michelle Obama Popularizes the Shift Dress

The shift dress is fast becoming as iconic as Diane von Furstenberg's wrap dress. The shift dress has been around since the 1920's and got a new lease of life in the 1960's when fashion icons such as Jackie O and Aubrey Hepburn constantly were pictured in them. Shift dresses being very simple to sew, became a housewife's wardrobe staple back in the 1960's as it was also easy to wear just skimming the body.

Shift dresses back on the fall 09 catwalks

Shift dresses were visible in many fall 2009 catwalk collections. This is due in part to its wearability as a garment in the light of a recession and more importantly due to the fact that it became Michelle Obama's signature look on the campaign trail. You need only Google "Michelle Obama shift dress" to see the many instances the First Lady worn this style dress in public More than the campaign trail, the First Lady wore a pale yellow shift dress and matching coat by Cuban born designer Isabel Toledo for the inauguration and was photographed in her first official portrait as First Lady in a classic sleeveless black shift dress designed by Michael Kors. The style needed no more endorsement than that to inspire a comeback on the catwalks.

Get the look - Michelle Obama's signature look

The key to Michelle Obama's popularization of the look is that she wore many affordable off the rack shift styles that the average woman who liked the look could go out and buy to recreate her signature look. Getting the look was easy as not only is it a look that is easy to wear and easy to recreate but there are many variations of the shift dress ranging from high end to low end. Michelle Obama made it okay for masses of women (fashion conscious or not) to comfortably wear low end ready to wear garments and feel like they were wearing high-end designer fashion as endorsed by Michelle Obama herself. Some of her off the rack choices came from high street shops such as H&M, J Crew and bouti☐ues such as Donna Ricco. Other top fashion designer names worn by Michelle Obama include Thakoon Panichgul, Maria Pinto and Narcisco Rodriguez.

The shift dress - a simple look ☐uietly accessorized with bold statement jewelery

Other than the classic pearls worn by Michelle Obama to accessorize Michael Kors black sleeveless shift dress in her first official portrait as First Lady, she opted for statement brooches and chunky bracelets to accessorize and pull looks together. Her large floral brooch in tur☐uoise I must say is my favorite so far.

Feminism- Why Michelle Obama is Like a Thief

Michelle Obama stole hopelessness from black women in exchange for hope. Hope to realize that high profile black men can really love and appreciate a black woman, and be proud to be with her. That not all high profile, black men are embarrassed to have a black woman as their wife.

Women, the answer is to educate yourself so that you don't need a man to feel complete. Basically, the man should be your partner and your companion.

Michelle stole the perception from most high profile black men that black women cannot be sexy and at the same time glamorous, sophisticated, intelligent and powerful. She is the representation of brains, glamor, and beauty, inside and outside. She is the First Lady of The United States of America.

No matter what happens in your life to make you feel inferior, don't let it get you down. Stand tall and be proud of who you are. Continue to look glamorous and remember, you are the First Lady of your home.

Michelle stole most black athletes' idea of a trophy wife, by showing them women who look like their black mothers and black sisters are beautiful. She stole their inferior complex and gave them self-confidence. Don't let society dictate to you who or what beauty is. You have to accept and love yourself before you can love someone else.

Michelle Obama stole the excuse from women and people of color who say they cannot accomplish anything because of the color of their skin or because they are A woman. She is very accomplished in her career and in her marriage. Her husband President Barack Obama said that Michelle is his rock.

Excuses are replaced with drive, enthusiasm, and determination. In life, you have to set goals and visualize yourself in that role. Use determination and drive as your guide to success.

Michelle stole the ideology that women have to hold high profile jobs outside the home to be recognized and respected. She has shown that women can have high profile jobs working from home. Working from home is great especially when you have small children.

Ensure that it is your choice if you choose to work outside the home, and you are not doing it to be respected by society. You should do it because you feel that it is the right thing to do for you, your children and your lifestyle.

Michelle stole the stigma that you have to wear designer clothes to be recognized and valued. She replaced that by wearing clothes from stores were regular American women shop. Michelle Obama gives women the confidence to feel proud and walk proud, even if you are not rich. Use her experience to do the right things in life, even if you are pressured and criticized.

Thanks for being a thief. Michelle, you have given black women the confidence to realize that they are beautiful. You have no idea how much of a large difference you have made in the lives of many women of color. You have helped black women everywhere feel a sense of beauty and confidence. Michelle, you are loved.

CHAPTER 4- SURPRISING FACTS ABOUT MICHELLE OBAMA

You've watched her on the campaign trail promoting Barack, but what do you really know about Michelle Obama? Here are facts you need to know about the First Lady:

1. Michelle LaVaughn Robinson was born Jan. 17, 1964, to Fraser and Marian Robinson. The family lived on the South Side of Chicago, and Fraser worked for the Chicago water department. Michelle attended the Whitney M. Young Magnet School.

2. Michelle followed her brother to Princeton University, where she graduated in 1985 with a bachelor's in sociology and a minor in African-American studies. For her thesis, "Princeton-Educated Blacks and the Black Community," she surveyed black alumni on their racial attitudes since graduating.

3. Michelle then attended Harvard Law School, earning her degree in 1988. After law school, she went to work at the Chicago law firm of Sidley & Austin.

4. At the law firm, she met Barack Obama. He was a summer associate; she was his adviser. While Michelle wasn't initially interested in a romance, she soon changed her mind. On their first date, Michelle and Barack saw Spike Lee's Do the Right Thing.

5. In the early 1990s, following the death of both her father and a close friend from college, Michelle reassessed her life. Rethinking her career path, she decided to leave the corporate law world to work in public service. She took a job in the mayor's office and then in the city's office of planning and development. In 1993, Michelle became the founding executive director of Public Allies Chicago,

an AmeriCorps national service program that provided training to young adults pursuing careers in the public sector.

6. In 1996, Michelle moved to a position with the University of Chicago. By 2005, she had worked her way up to a vice president spot at the University Medical Center.

7. Barack Obama's career was launched into the national spotlight when he delivered a speech at the 2004 Democratic National Convention. On his way to the stage, Michelle reportedly gave him a hug and told him (breaking the tension): "Just don't screw it up, buddy."

8. Michelle and Barack have been married since October 1992. The couple has two young daughters: Malia and Sasha.

9. The Obamas work hard to give their daughters a grounded life. When Obama was on the road as a senator, they used webcams to see and talk to one another.

10. Michelle is a Stevie Wonder fan, and exercise is a favorite hobby (she reportedly used to get up at 4:30 a.m. to run on a treadmill).

11. Even though she's supermodel tall (5'11"!), Michelle didn't go out for the basketball team in high school. Instead, she was involved with student government, the choir, and organizing school plays.

12. According to Barack, Michelle doesn't like to play Scrabble. Why? She's very competitive, he says, and "I usually beat her, and I tend to gloat." (Oprah)

13. She loves French fries.

CHAPTER 5- HOW MICHELLE OBAMA BECAME MORE THAN JUST ANOTHER POLITICAL VOIC

When Michelle Obama delivered the most influential speech of the 2016 campaign in an out-of-the-way stop in New Hampshire, she suddenly and somewhat unexpectedly commanded the spotlight with her emotional account of how Donald Trump's private words about women's bodies had "shaken me to my core."

Though she spoke earlier that month while much of the country was seeing for the first time video of Trump's lewd bragging, the first lady actually had been working on the address for weeks, incorporating her growing concern about the GOP presidential nominee's many insults of women into a polemic that drew from her own experiences of being verbally harassed on the street and ogled at work.

"I feel it so personally." she said. "The shameful comments about our bodies. The disrespect of our ambitions and intellect. The belief that you can do anything you want to a woman."

Trump's attitude toward women had been "weighing on her for a long time," one senior adviser said. "She wanted to speak about it."

The speech, amplified by timing and met with an enthusiastic response, cemented Obama's place as a star of the presidential race and put a defining stroke not just on how women view Trump but on herself as a voice of moral authority. Three months before leaving the White House, she already is among the ranks of public figures who transcend politics and title.

She's variously called an "icon," one of "the greats" and a woman who "changed history" in an essay collection in the current issue of the New York Times' "T" magazine, titled "To the First Lady, with Love."

"When you rise to a level like that, you see how much weight your words carry," said Anita McBride, former chief of staff to First Lady Laura Bush and executive in residence at the School of Public Affairs at American University. "We know she didn't like politics. But she was impassioned by the language that was used, and she feels compelled to speak out. People listen to her."

For Obama, it was an uphill climb to that moment. She was reticent to get involved in campaigns early on, suspecting that they were difficult for a family.

"Michelle was never wild about politics," President Obama told late-night host Jimmy Kimmel. When he was thinking of running for president, he said, his wife told him, "You would make an outstanding president, and I would work so hard to make sure you were president ... if I weren't married to you."

Her fears proved prescient in the 2008 Democratic primary, when a fierce stereotype of her as an angry black woman developed. A cartoon on the cover of the New Yorker pictured her in militant garb.

She pulled out of the campaign for weeks, emerging later with a bold and disciplined new branding plan that included careful decisions about what she said in interviews and to whom she said it. She since has favored women's and celebrity magazines and friendly television venues over straight news outlets.

Democrats must win four seats and the presidency to reclaim Senate control

And at the heart of her strategy is a cautious defense of her time. She takes care to leave plenty of it for her teenage daughters — but also to place a premium on when she appears in the spotlight.

While her husband and Vice President Joseph Biden were starting to publicly back former secretary of State Hillary Clinton at the beginning of the summer as she closed in on the Democratic presidential nomination, Michelle

Obama mostly held her fire until the Democratic National Convention at the end of July.

When she did take the stage, Democrats who remembered the enmity between the Obama and Clinton camps in 2008 were rapt, listening to see how hard she would lean into the endorsement.

Obama did not worry about selling her lines, one adviser said. She has developed a deep respect for her East Wing predecessor.

"I trust Hillary to lead this country," Obama said, "because I've seen her lifelong devotion to our nation's children, not just her own daughter, who she has raised to perfection."

Her pitch has been similarly personal on the campaign trail, where Obama has been available more than Clinton campaign officials anticipated.

The race to 270: Which states are in play?

At one event, she said of Clinton that "when she gets knocked down … she doesn't complain." For emphasis, Obama tapped her mic — a reference to Trump's complaints that his microphone had not been working properly at the first presidential debate. The wordless put-down went viral.

"She's particularly effective because she's not viewed as someone who lives in the day-to-day political battles," said Jennifer Palmieri, a top adviser to the Clinton campaign. "They don't see her in the daily tumult."

Indeed, Obama's positioning of herself as far outside of politics as is possible for a first lady has helped mute criticism and contributed to a perception that she is above the fray.

Republicans have been sparing, if sharp, in their criticism of her. After she said Trump exhibited "sexually predatory behavior" in bragging about grabbing women in the "Access Hollywood" video from 2005, Trump's running mate, Indiana Gov. Mike Pence, said he didn't understand the basis of her claim.

"What he's made clear," Pence said of Trump, "is that was talk, regrettable talk, on his part, but that there were no actions."

Trump fired off critical tweets about other speakers at the Democratic convention but was mum on Michelle Obama. A GOP spokesman said, "The first lady is off-limits."

Later, Trump complained about an implicit shot Obama took at Clinton during the 2008 primaries, though the first lady has denied she was targeting her husband's then-rival.

This fall, she has made it clear to White House aides that she didn't just want to take on Trump, she wanted to take a stand for women and girls — and for Clinton in particular.

At their first joint campaign event, in a North Carolina arena packed with 11,000 supporters, Obama acknowledged that it's "unprecedented" for a first lady to campaign as much as she has

"That may be true," she said. "But this is also an unprecedented election."

Abio Harris, 54, and Yvette Jones, 57, who work together at a local non-profit, like Clinton. But they love Obama.

"Michelle is very deep," Jones said. "She can take things to a different level."

Harris was effusive. "I love FLOTUS," she said, referring to Obama by the Washington shorthand for first lady of the United States. "She represents the best of the administration."

CHAPTER 6- MICHELLE ON LEADERSHIP

The 9 systems of leadership are relational, psychological, leverage of power, leverage of skill, negotiation, sacrifice, responsibility, living in paradox, and vision. Michelle Obama's Democratic National Convention speech effectively and seamlessly touched on the leadership system which is why her speech has been revered by the public and critics alike.

Relational

Her speech began with forming a connection and her perspective and life experience is relatable to 99% of all Americans. We understand the American struggle and the perseverance our ancestors displayed in desperate times for survival. She touched on a common connection that we all share and explained how she and her family share the same existence.

Psychological

Leadership is psychological and enlightened by the ability to manage the stress of others caused by changing times. She told stories that incited strong emotions related to challenging situations that her family and the American people have experienced. She expressed her understanding of these situations and how they as a family have dealt with these experiences in the past. She explained how President Obama does not flinch in times of challenge, but rather, he moves forward with wisdom and compassion.

Leverage Power and Skill

Leadership leverages power to provide for the needs of others by creating security, individual respect for the self and for others, an aura of acceptance and unity, the spirit of love, by creating meaning opportunities, and encouraging achievement. Michelle Obama spoke about the foundation of her family which is love. Love is the central mandatory theme for all successful leadership. A leader without love is a castle without furniture. Michelle Obama vividly showed through her speech that love to her family is everything. She expressed that their love is strong - strong enough to share with the world. By diffusion, these concepts led to inspiration for many Americans and non-Americans around the world because her speech spoke to the fact that her and her husband started from humble beginnings. She spoke to the meaning of hard work and belief in a greater good. The concept of giving back and not shutting the door on others is an American value that we all need to embrace and giving back was central to Obama's leadership.

Negotiation

Michelle's calm demeanor is evidence of her high-level of self-awareness and superior confidence in her truth. She and her husband have shown the ability to control their emotions during difficult times and be incredibly accepting of conflicting feedback. These abilities are the skills that all leaders need in order to be successful. Michelle spoke strongly about her family values and how they align with American values. Leadership values depend on the culture it leads and the alignment of these values is essential to gain buy-in from the public at large.

Negotiating a situation with a steadfast commitment to values predicts choices during complexity. She spoke about the most difficult situations crossing the President's desk and there being no justification for a specific right or a wrong answer. She explained that these pressure-driven choices are made based on the values the President holds and that his values are the same as America's values. This concept enables the American public to embody the President's mentality during difficult decision-making and develop a level of empathy because people could relate to the thought-process involved.

Sacrifice

Leadership is sacrifice and Michelle spoke about Barack not accepting higher paying positions in exchange for advocating for peoples' rights because it was the right thing to do. President Obama has shown the mandatory motivation to be a successful leader. He has stood strong for something meaning to others for most of his political career. Servant leadership builds trust and trust mediates the speed of success. Her speech was geared at regaining the trust they have lost through conflicting allegations that have portrayed their leadership in negative light. Michelle spoke about the sincerity they feel for the American people and the sacrifice that her family has made in order to obtain their leadership position. She spoke about the concern she had for her family adapting to the national spotlight.

Responsibility

Leadership is responsibility and without responsibility there is no leadership. The position of the President of the United States comes with the most situational responsibility in the world. Leaders accept large amounts of responsibility and thrive when the pressure is on. Michelle Obama spoke about enacting the new healthcare law and the responsibility President Obama felt that enabled him to make the difficult choices that were needed to complete the passing of the law. President Obama also took responsibility for the passing of the Equal Pay Act and repealing Don't Ask Don't Tell. These are controversial issues that are highly contested, but President Obama took a stand for what he believed was right based on his values system. Michelle spoke about the enormous responsibility that President Obama felt for the American people and the successes that were achieved because of the circumstances.

Paradox

Leadership is about living in paradox - living in moments of complete uncertainty with no clear answers - the "damned if you do and damned if you don't" moments. Leadership is full of these moments and accepting an imperfect existence is essential to leading with a clear mind and a clear heart. Dwelling on past events or concern for current ambiguous situations greatly decrease leadership ability. A successful leader uses these paradoxical situations to inspire action and commitment through calmness and honesty. Leaders like Lincoln and Washington were masters of paradox and Michelle spoke about the challenges that faced the Obama leadership over the duration of the presidency. The challenges were vast and complicated. They were compared to the previous presidential challenges of Teddy Roosevelt during the Great Depression and the contention and confrontation of the GOP during every step of Obama's leadership. These were some of the paradoxical dilemmas that his administration faced.

Vision

Leadership is vision and Michelle Obama spoke about Barack Obama's vision from when they first met and how it has evolved overtime. She spoke about his vision having a foundation in American values and his belief in the strength of America. His vision includes the opportunity for a superior education for everyone, the ability to get proper healthcare when needed, and the ability to live the American dream for all. She spoke of the vision of the next generation being greater than us and having the opportunity to provide for the vision. The vision is full of inspiration, commitment, concern, love, opportunity, empowerment, responsibility, and unity to make the vision a reality.

Michelle Obama is a great leader. Without Michelle there is no Barack. She is the foundation of their family and showed her strength and courage in front of hundreds of millions of people from around the world. In my opinion, she deserves the title of America's first lady and has lived up to the title with style, grace, and leadership.

CONCLUSION

Michelle Obama, or more formally known as Michelle LaVaughn Robinson Obama is the much loved wife and first lady of the former president of the United States, Barack Obama. She has been known only by this address to most people; though the woman behind the name is one who has been strong, loving and determined throughout her life. She has attended Princeton University where she majored in Sociology and has minored in African American studies and has graduated cum laude. She then moved forward to Harvard Law School where she obtained her J.D or Juris Doctor Degree. Ever since, this woman has always been an advocate for e□uality and for humanitarian projects. She has served mainly around the Chicago area where she took on positions to serve students and the community as she has eventually boarded the train for the administration of the University of Chicago Hospitals.

The Michelle Obama Effect

The lines have been drawn in the sand and consumer brands and their pr teams better sit up and take notice. For years affluent African-American moms have been crying foul regarding campaigns that show them as loud, brash, cold, and bossy. Until now their grumbles have been relatively contained to the beauty salons, churches, and at Sunday family dinners. Black moms have remained vexed and embarrassed by the portrayal of them as one of two models; either ebonic-speaking, booty shakin', sex-pots, or, ignorant, obese, and domineering. Black moms have been troubled by this depiction in mainstream media but have remained relatively silent in communicating those frustrations publicly- until now.

The world held its breath as Americans elected Senator Barack Obama as the 44th President of the United States in 2008. In President-Elect Barack

Obama's acceptance speech he gave a short but moving tribute to his African-American wife, partner, biggest supporter, and mother of his children, Mrs. Michelle Obama. Black women across the country wept at such a public expression of love and respect for a woman whose physical image reflects their own. Some have never witnessed such an outpouring of affection over an entire lifetime. Finally the world was seeing an educated, nurturing, accomplished mother who looks, talks, and shares the same goals, values, and aspirations as them. For the first time, on the world stage was a Black woman that seemed so familiar; someone who could fit in easily at a book club or at the local Mocha Mom or Jack and Jill group. The minute Michelle Obama came on the national scene the passive stance of Black mom consumers changed. Black moms are now chanting "No more!", and they are putting their purses where their mouths are. This is indeed the Michelle Obama Effect.

So what is the Michelle Obama Effect and what does it mean to practitioners? It means change. It means African-American moms taking control of their image and rejecting brands that reduce them to stereotypes and caricatures. And most importantly, it means that practitioners are going to have to develop pr and marketing programs that represent African-American moms in very real and relevant ways. Otherwise practitioners will watch these traditionally brand loyal moms exercise the power of their purses by switching to competing brands.

In 2011 African-American families were expected to spend an estimated 1 trillion dollars a year. Black moms make 87% of the purchasing decisions for products for their homes. Unless brands are willing to forsake their stake in this trillion dollar market, practitioners should treat the Michelle Obama Effect as a genuine and extremely significant movement.

Michelle Obama Diet - Secrets to a Buff Body and Arms

Michelle Obama in contrast to most Democrats is conservative -- we are not talking about politics here -- we are referring to Michelle Obamas diet program of course . In a recent article in women's health magazine. Mrs. Obama revealed her "secrets" to maintaining her weight, health and having a lean -- yet toned body. It all stems from her upbringing... when she was growing up McDonald's was a very rare treat. Consequently, she developed a healthy attitude towards diet and food

However, Michelle Obama still has weaknesses -- her favorite food in the whole wide world is... French Fries!

Her diet secret is really nothing new it is -- MODERATION. She attempts to make good choices when it comes to food as often as possible yet she will indulge herself on occasion. So while she may not eat an entire pound of french fries -- she will occasionally have them.

Her personal trainer Cornell McClellan has been helping Mrs. Obama stay in shape since 1997. The Michelle Obama workout consists of strength training, cardiovascular exercise (running, walking on a treadmill etc.) and flexibility training.

She will also on occasion mix up her cardio workouts by including kickboxing and calisthenics.

Mrs. Obama is not the only one in her family with a passion for fitness... recently President Obama was named one of the top 25 "Fittest Guys in America" by Men's Fitness Magazine. One of the Obama diet secrets is that they both have eliminated junk food from their diets and added organic foods and vegetables.

The secrets to losing weight is all about calories. 1 pound is e ual to 3500 calories so if you are looking to lose weight merely reduce your caloric intake by 500 calories and if you will add in 45 minutes to one hour of cardio you will burn an additional 500 calories. That will put you on pace to losing approximately 2 pounds per week.

You must include resistance training into your workouts to ensure that you lose body fat and not muscle. Women want to retain as much muscle on their body as possible... muscle is what gives your body those curves and shape that every woman wants.

The Michelle Obama diet is really just about common sense -- all things in moderation -- eliminate junk food -- eat healthy food and exercise regularly.

Michelle Obama - The Fashionable Star of America

Time is flying; every day, every people, every country experiences different things. However, as human beings, we should not just pursue the future. Sometimes we need to slow down our steps to relax ourselves; then we can memorize some important things which we had enjoyed. As American, do you still remember what happened on January, 20th, 2009? That is a great day for Americans, especially for Obama and Michelle Obama.

On January, 20th, 2009, the new America President Obama's official inauguration party was held in Washington; they were the protagonists of that party. As usual, Obama had put on his beloved parity suit, and then have you paid your attention to the dress of Michelle Obama? Wow! She was the star of that party, and she so gorgeous; and every one was shocked by her dress. She had attended the memorial significant party with the white Beautify One-Shoulder Floor-length Prom Evening Dress. Compare to the dress which was designed by Isabel Toledo at the Inauguration ceremony, this white dress made Michelle Obama look much younger, and more attractive. On the party, when the new president Obama talked with the guests, he showed his appreciation to her directly, and made a joke with the guests, "how gorgeous my wife is!", and all the people were issued to give hearty laugh by his words.

The first lady Michelle Obama is good at tie-in dress. She likes dressing with mix style, so she always uses the clothes which you bought from the store to match with the clothes which was designed by her own designer. No matter where is she, she can always show us her perfect dress style. And she has great impact to the fashion world, the related information as following:

1. In the talk show "The View", as she wore a skirt which values $148, then alot of America women tried to get that kind of skirt.

2. Since she wore the H&M skirt when she attended one important occasion, then we all understood that sometimes you can also have your own style without spending too much money.

3. After she wore the skirt which was designed by a new designer, and then this lucky designer soon becomes a newly popular star in fashion world.

4. The white Beautify One-Shoulder Floor-length Prom Evening Dress which she wore on the inauguration party was designed by the Jason Wu. After this important occasion, this designer becomes the focus of public concern immediately, and now he has expanded his own designed style.

5. On the "Tonight Show", Michelle Obama wore the shoes of J.Crew, as the result, the high-heeled shoes of this brand increased 64% on sales' aspect.

Wow! Have you shocked by these great influences of Michelle Obama? Michelle Obama is not only the first lady of America but also the fashionable star in the fashion world. If you want to be more fashionable, you may pay more attention to this great lady!

Backstage with Michelle and Barack Obama

After eight years of living at the epicenter of a tightly controlled bubble, Barack and Michelle Obama seem to savor the little things most now that their historic White House tenure has ended.

For Michelle, it's the chance to pop into a Soul Cycle class, pack her own bag lunch (turkey chili is a favorite) and eat with her staff while laughing over viral videos in their new work space in D.C.'s West End, where her office is painted the same warm salmon pink of her old East Wing digs.

For Barack, it's the opportunity to dust off the leather jacket that stayed hidden in his closet for years because he didn't think it was presidential enough to wear while in office.

"Imagine putting on a suit and tie almost every day for eight years. I think he enjoys not having to do that," Barack's chief of staff, Anita Breckenridge, tells PEOPLE in this week's issue, which offers an inside look at the former first couple's post-White House life.

But exclusive images of the former president and former first lady— already making quiet visits to Washington, D.C. schools, and speeches on higher education and health care—show that neither one is ready to retire.

Says longtime friend Marty Nesbitt, who now chairs the Obama Foundation: "They had always been engaged citizens working to help improve the lives of the people around them and the presidency was a part of that continuum. Their lives don't end after his presidency ended and so they energized by the opportunity to be private citizens again."

The end

22851582R00027

Printed in Great Britain
by Amazon